I LOVE CATS

Barney Saltzberg

CANDLEWICK PRESS
CAMBRIDGE, MASSACHUSETTS

I love cats.

Stripy
cats.

Spotted
cats.

Cats
that
count
drips.

Climbing
cats.

Scaredy
cats.

Cats
that
do
flips.

Cats
that
chase
shadows

or curl up
like a ball.

Tail
or
no
tail,

I love
them
all.

Some cats just yawn.

Some cats just purr.

Some cats
just watch.

And some clean their fur.

I love cats that hide.

I love cats that peep.

I love cats
that dream

kitty dreams
as they sleep.

It isn't their whiskers,

their meow,

or their mew. . . .

I love cats.